HAL•LEONARD®
RECORDER
SONGBOOK

Christmas Hits

T0081321

ISBN 978-1-4803-9313-4

HAL•LEONARD®
CORPORATION
7777 W. BLUEMOUND RD. P.O. BOX 13819 MILWAUKEE, WI 53213

Visit Hal Leonard Online at
www.halleonard.com

BLUE CHRISTMAS

RECORDER

Words and Music by BILLY HAYES
and JAY JOHNSON

CHRISTMAS IS A-COMIN'
(May God Bless You)

RECORDER

Words and Music by
FRANK LUTHER

DO YOU HEAR WHAT I HEAR

RECORDER

Words and Music by NOEL REGNEY
and GLORIA SHAYNE

FROSTY THE SNOW MAN

RECORDER

Words and Music by STEVE NELSON
and JACK ROLLINS

GROWN-UP CHRISTMAS LIST

RECORDER

Words and Music by DAVID FOSTER
and LINDA THOMPSON-JENNER

HAPPY HOLIDAY

from the Motion Picture Irving Berlin's HOLIDAY INN

RECORDER

Words and Music by
IRVING BERLIN

HERE COMES SANTA CLAUS
(Right Down Santa Claus Lane)

RECORDER

Words and Music by GENE AUTRY
and OAKLEY HALDEMAN

(There's No Place Like)
HOME FOR THE HOLIDAYS

RECORDER

Words and Music by AL STILLMAN
and ROBERT ALLEN

I SAW MOMMY KISSING SANTA CLAUS

RECORDER

Words and Music by
TOMMIE CONNOR

JINGLE BELL ROCK

RECORDER

Words and Music by JOE BEAL
and JIM BOOTHE

THE LITTLE DRUMMER BOY

RECORDER

Words and Music by HARRY SIMEONE,
HENRY ONORATI and KATHERINE DAVIS

Moderately slow, in 2

MISTLETOE AND HOLLY

RECORDER

Words and Music by FRANK SINATRA,
DOK STANFORD and HENRY W. SANICOLA

WHITE CHRISTMAS
from the Motion Picture Irving Berlin's HOLIDAY INN

RECORDER

Words and Music by
IRVING BERLIN

WINTER WONDERLAND

RECORDER

Words by DICK SMITH
Music by FELIX BERNARD

YOU'RE ALL I WANT FOR CHRISTMAS

RECORDER

Words and Music by GLEN MOORE
and SEGER ELLIS